A GUIDED

Prayer Journey

A JOURNAL FOR
WRITING PERSONALIZED
PRAYERS that avail much

A GUIDED

Prayer Journey

A JOURNAL FOR
WRITING PERSONALIZED
PRAYERS that avail much

Germaine Copeland

Prayers are paraphrased from the above-listed Bible versions and excerpted from *Prayers That Avail Much 40th Anniversary Edition, Prayers That Avail Much to Overcome Anxiety and Depression,* and *Prayers That Avail Much for Leaders.*

Dictionary definitions cited from Merriam-webster.com.

Prayers That Avail Much® is a registered trademark of Word Ministries, Inc., a Georgia corporation.

Compiled and edited by Kaye Hoole Mountz

Published by Harrison House Publishers
Shippensburg, PA 17257

This book and all other Destiny Image and Destiny Image Fiction books are available at Christian bookstores and distributors worldwide.

For more information on foreign distributors, call 717-532-3040.

Reach us on the Internet: www.destinyimage.com.

ISBN 13 TP: 978-1-6675-0002-7

For Worldwide Distribution, Printed in the U.S.A.

1 2 3 4 5 6 7 8 / 26 25 24 23 22

prayer

pray·er | \ ˈprā-ər, ˈprer \
A petition to God; a set order of words

journey

jour·ney | \ ˈjər-nē \ plural journeys
noun—travel or passage from
one place to another, to go on a
journey, to travel over or through

Your prayer journey
is about to begin.

Contents

The earnest prayer of a righteous man has great power and wonderful results.
—James 5:16 TLB

A Letter from Germaine

Dear Friend,

Let's begin a journey in the pages that follow that will change your prayer life, and as a result, change your entire life.

At 88 years of age, I'm so grateful for what the Lord has taught me about prayer and honored that He has graced me to write more than 50 books on the topic. But the most valuable prayer I can compose is the one that teaches you how to write your own prayer. The circumstances, challenges, heartbreaks, desires, and hopes that come along for you are so vast and complex that the best person to write prayers for you is *you!*

On this prayer journey, you will develop a more intimate relationship with God, allowing Him to take charge and direct your prayers. The journey will become even more exciting as you learn to articulate your thoughts and feelings, apply the Word of God, and encase it all in faith-filled words to your heavenly Father who delivers great power and wonderful results (James 5:16 TLB). That is prayer that avails much! And that is your journey that begins now....

Your partner in prayer,

Germaine

How to Build Prayers That Avail Much

Effective, fervent prayers that avail much don't just happen—they are built on the firm foundation of God's Word. Even then, while prayer should be a comfortable and heartfelt conversation with the One who knows you best and loves you most, the only way to pray God's will is to build your prayer on God's Word because God *is* His Word (John 1:1, 2 Tim. 3:16-17, John 1:14). God wants your prayers to avail much, and that's why He tells you exactly how to pray.

First John 5:14-15 says, "Now this is the confidence that we have in Him, that if we ask anything according to His will, He hears us. And if we know that He hears us, whatever we ask, we know that we have the petitions that we have asked of Him" (NKJV). That's a pretty ironclad guarantee! So, let's take a closer at how to sharpen your prayer skills, whether you are a beginner pray-er or a seasoned pray-er.

God Created You to Pray

God designed man from the beginning to fellowship with Him, and prayer is just an outflow of the relationship He desires with every believer. Your heavenly Father wants to talk to *you*. You can *know* God and tell Him anything and everything! God is Spirit, and the real you is a spirit. In fact, 1 Thessalonians 5:23 explains you are spirit who has a soul and lives in a body of flesh. But it's your spirit that communicates with God—the real you who will live eternally.

When you received Jesus as your Lord and Savior, God raised the real you from the dead and made you alive in Christ. Now, spiritually speaking, you are seated in heavenly places with Him (Eph. 2). In 2 Peter 1:1-4, Peter outlines how you are a partaker of this divine nature and by faith you are able to ignite the power God has imparted to you. You learn to talk with your Father using words that are spirit and life—supernatural words found in the book we call the Bible.

This passage in 2 Peter also tells us that God has *already blessed* you with exceedingly great and precious promises, and through faith and prayer, you take hold of them. You learn who God is and who you are in Christ Jesus. When the enemy comes to sow doubt, you will have an arsenal of weapons. God's Word written on the tablet of your heart is your sword against any attempt of the devil to steal, kill, and destroy (John 10:10). Satan does not play by the rules, and he will attempt to convince you that you do not have time to pray. But Jesus came to earth to teach us how to live, and Jesus is a pray-er. Jesus also showed us in Matthew 4 how to stare down Lucifer: with the Word.

The Holy Spirit is present to help you pray when you do not know how or what to pray (Rom. 8:26). As you renew your mind to the Word of God and set your mind on things above, you learn the strategies of prayer, the different forms of prayer, and with the help of the Holy Spirit, prayer becomes as natural and vital as breathing.

When you were born again by the Spirit of God, He awakened your spirit and gave you the ability to communicate with Him through His Word. God talks with you through the pages of the Bible. Prayer is a conversation with the Creator of the universe who also just happens to be your Father. Praying scriptural prayer is praying the language of heaven. You will learn God's thoughts that are higher than yours, and therefore, prayers based on His words will know no limitations. Your faith will increase as you hear yourself speaking His words and thoughts in your prayers. Furthermore, God watches over His Word to perform it (Jer. 1:12) and not one word of His good promise has ever failed to come to pass (1 Kngs. 8:56).

Seven Building Blocks of Strong Prayer

Let's look at the seven building blocks of prayers that avail much.

Building Block #1—Your prayer time is a conversation with God who loves you unconditionally. So be real and speak from your heart. You don't need to be on your knees, you don't need to fold your hands, and you don't need thee's and thou's.

Your number one resource for what to say is the Bible. God talks to you from His written Word, and you can do the same.

If you are at a loss for words, you might turn to a scripture and pray from it. For example, you could turn to Psalm 42:1 and pray, "As the deer longs for streams of water, so I long for You, O God." Pray in first person or insert the names of people for whom you are praying. Prayer is not about many words or eloquent words. It's about Word-based, heart-to-heart conversation with your Father-God.

Scriptural prayers usher you into a greater intimacy with the Creator. God reveals His will, His mind, and His thoughts to you, and you learn to speak His language. Over-time, you will find yourself talking to Him throughout the day—just as you would any very close friend.

Throughout the pages that follow, we've provided guides and cues to help you learn to pray or deepen and expand your prayers. At the end of each of three sections, we've also included pages where you decide what you pray about and you can personalize this journey even more specifically. Remember, this is *your* journal for your eyes only, so express yourself freely!

Building Block #2—Pray to the Father in Jesus' name (John 14:13-14). This is an important opening and closing line, but it's also much more. In Colossians 3:17, Paul says, "And whatever you do, in word or deed, do everything in the name of the Lord Jesus, giving thanks to God the Father through him." That includes prayer! ***Prayer*** is an action verb, and when we pray, we enter into agreement with Him. Jesus is seated at the right hand of the Father praying for you, and Ephesians 2 says you are seated together with Him in heavenly places. That means the devil is under your feet (along with whatever problem he might bring your way).

From the moment you pray, "Dear Father," you are accessing the throne room. Your Father is listening, and you are taking your position in Him in prayer—above whatever problem you're praying about.

When you pray in Jesus' name, you "seal the deal" with the blood of Jesus that purchased the answer to your prayer. Jesus' name is the authority that allows you to say "amen" or "so be it."

Building Block #3—As we've discussed, God tells you how to pray in 1 John 5:14-15, where He makes the Word a priority in prayer. The Word lays a firm foundation for whatever you will ask.

Look up scriptures that speak to your situation or prayer request. Perhaps read the verses in different Bible versions because different wording can sometimes provide new insight. If you don't know the meaning of a particular word or the Holy Spirit highlights a word to you, look it up online or in a concordance (Strong's concordance is my favorite). We've listed resources on page 191 to help you with this. It's easy to quickly look up multiple Bible versions by visiting www.biblegateway.com or www.biblehub.com.

Even if you are well acquainted with the scriptures, still look up words that apply to your situation to allow God's Word to speak to you. As an example: If you are praying to overcome fear, look up the word *fear* and find scriptures where it appears. The Word of God will enlighten you with revelation, energize you, give you confidence, and build your faith (Rom. 10:17).

Building Block #4—Pray believing! (Mark 11:24). In Romans 1:16, Paul says, "For I am not ashamed of the gospel of Christ, for it is the power of God to salvation for everyone who *believes*." Notice that believing in the gospel or God's Word ignites the power! Our prayers are built on the fact that we trust God to keep His promises (Num. 23:19; 1 Kngs. 8:56).

Building Block #5—Your words have power. Proverbs 18:21 says you have the power of life and death in your tongue, so speak life! After praying God's Word about a matter, do not waver by talking about the problem afterward. Don't pray one thing and leave prayer discussing the problem with others. Act like the Word is true because it is (James 2:17).

Building Block #6—Praise God *before* you see the answer to your prayer. Praise God because you see the answer through your spiritual eyes—through the eye of faith. Praise is the highest kind of prayer and your faith in action. It also silences the enemy who tries to steal your joy (Heb. 13:15). Do not be moved by what you see with your natural eyes. When doubt tries to take root, get your written prayer out, and declare every word with praise.

Building Block #7—In Luke 17, Jesus healed 10 lepers but only one returned to thank Him. Be that thankful one!

Thank God for answered prayer. Keeping a journal and filling out the "My Praise Report" will help you remember how your prayers were answered. Be thankful and say so with great joy. It is your Father's joy to answer prayer, and remember, in His presence is fullness of joy for you.

On page 12, you will find a guide to help you make the most of this journal as well as cues to personalize it.

Most of all, friend, always remember you will learn the very most about prayer by praying!

Dissecting a Model Prayer

We've focused on the components of building strong prayers—the building blocks that every Word-based, faith-filled prayer must include. Now, let's focus on a prayer that Jesus Himself personally taught His disciples and us.

We often refer to this prayer in Matthew 6:9-13 as "The Lord's Prayer," because it is a model of how we should pray. Let's dissect it to see why.

That's King James for this is how to pray!

9 *After this manner therefore pray ye:*

Pray to the Father!

Our Father which art in heaven, Hallowed be thy name.

Praise Him who is far above your problem!

10 *Thy kingdom come, Thy will be done in earth, as it is in heaven.*

11 *Give us this day our daily bread.*

Establish your request solidly on God's Word!

12 *And forgive us our debts, as we forgive our debtors.*

Receive forgiveness from your Father and forgive others (Eph. 4:32). Forgiveness is a non-negotiable instruction. Mark 11:25 says when you pray, you must forgive. Always!

13 *And lead us not into temptation, but deliver us from evil: For thine is the kingdom, and the power, and the glory, forever.*

Again, we worship!

Amen.

Amen means "so be it!" So, going forward, immediately align your words with your faith-filled prayer! You cannot pray one thing and then talk another.

A Guide to Using and Personalizing This Journal

God's Word Speaking to Me

In this section, there are topical scriptures where God shares His thoughts and ways with you! Look up the scriptures in different Bible versions. Meditate on them, and make notes when the Holy Spirit personalizes them to you!

My Prayer

Here you'll find space to write prayers. I've written some prayers for you and only started others. In some instances, I've asked you to identify scriptures that compose a prayer. This will add depth to your prayers and bolster your faith to pray!

My Praise Report

Celebrate your victories and keep record of them in the space provided. It will encourage you and inspire faith-filled prayers in the future!

Reflection

Here you'll find a thought or scripture worthy of special focus!

Action

Here you'll discover exercises that call for declarations, probing questions that call for answers meant for your eyes only, or prompts that will give feet to your prayers!

Today, my prayer journey begins…

_____

(your name)

_____

(date)

…to God be the glory.

Prayers for Personal Growth

My Love Walk

> *...We can now experience the endless love of God cascading into our hearts through the Holy Spirit who lives in us!*
> —ROMANS 5:5 TPT

Reflection

Loving Is Always Right but not Always Easy

As believers, we're born of love, infused with love, and instructed by God Himself to love our neighbors as ourselves (Matt. 22:39). But what happens when our neighbor isn't so lovable? We must step out of our human love and into God's love—the personality of Love Himself.

Immerse yourself in these love scriptures and then find them in the prayer that follows. As you are meditating on these scriptures, make a few notes to yourself. All the while, the Holy Spirit will write them on the tablets of your heart!

God's Word Speaking to Me

Romans 5:5 TPT ❀ Philippians 1:9-11 ❀ 1 John 2:5 ❀ John 13:34 ❀ 1 John 4:8, 18 ❀ John 13:34 ❀ 1 Corinthians 13:4-8 TPT ❀ Daniel 1:9 AMPC ❀ Romans 12:14 AMPC ❀ Ephesians 3:17 AMPC ❀ Matthew 5:44 ❀ Romans 8:35-39

....

....

....

....

....

....

....

....

....

....

....

My Prayer

You'll notice how these scriptures below were weaved together to write this prayer!

Dear Father, thank You that Your love <u>has been poured forth into my heart</u> by the Holy Spirit

Romans 5:5

who has been given to me. I keep and treasure Your Word. The love of and for You,

1 John 2:5

Father, <u>has been perfected and completed</u> in me, and <u>perfect love casts out fear.</u>

1 John 4:18

I am born of love with love cascading in my heart, and I choose to love others that You have

1 John 13:34; Romans 5:5 TPT;

instructed me to love. You make me to find favor, compassion, and loving-kindness

Daniel 1:9 AMPC

Love does not traffic in shame and disrespect nor selfishly seek its own honor. I choose

1 Corinthians 13:4-8 TPT

to walk in the love of God that is not easily irritated or quick to take offense. I find no delight in what is wrong. Love is a safe place of shelter, and I will never stop believing the best for others even when I'm tempted. Love never takes failure as defeat, for it never gives up. I cannot control how others behave, but I can control my reaction. I choose to walk in love. As I stand praying, I choose to forgive those who have hurt or mistreated me.

Mark 11:25

My love abounds yet more and more in knowledge and in all judgment. I approve what is excellent, and I will be sincere and without offense till Jesus returns.

Philippians 1:9-11

I am rooted deep in love and founded securely on love,

Ephesians 3: 17 AMPC

knowing that nothing separates me from Your love. In Jesus' name, I pray. Amen.

John 14:13,   Romans 8:35-39

Action

Love Is an Act

How will you put love in action in your life?

1. _____

2. _____

3. _____

4. _____

5. _____

6. _____

7. _____

8. _____

9. _____

10. _____

11. _____

12. _____

My Praise Report

Forgiveness

*Whenever you stand praying, if you have any-thing against anyone, forgive him and **let it drop (leave it, let it go)**, in order that your Father Who is in heaven may also forgive you your [own] failings and shortcomings and let them drop.*
—MARK 11:25 AMPC

Reflection

To Err is Human—to Forgive Is Downright Supernatural

There isn't a human alive who hasn't been hurt, mistreated, or annoyed by another. Sometimes these wounds are as heartbreaking as being deliberately stabbed in the back or as minor as a coworker with an irksome habit. Either way, the Bible makes no distinction between the two but simply commands us to forgive.

Let's get real! Who do you need to forgive, and what do you need to drop, leave, and let go?

God's Word Speaking to Me

Romans 12:16-18 ❋ Mark 11:25 ❋ Romans 12:10 ❋ Ephesians 4:31-32 ❋ Philippians 2:21 ❋ Peter 3:8,11-12 ❋ Colossians 1:10 ❋ Romans 5:5 ❋ John 1:9 ❋ Philippians 1:9,11 ❋ 2 Corinthians 2:10-12 TPT

....

....

....

....

My Prayer

I'll start, and you finish!

Dear Father, I realize from Your Word that forgiveness is a choice, and today I choose to…

....

....

....

....

....

....

....

....

Reflection

Even As

"And be kind to one another, tenderhearted, forgiving one another, *even as* God in Christ forgave you" (Eph. 4:32). Ouch! Those two little words "even as" can really step on toes. How will you go forward tenderheartedly?

....
....
....
....
....
....
....
....

My Praise Report

....
....
....
....
....
....

Looking Like Jesus

> *...Until we are unified in faith and filled with the knowledge of the Son of God, until we stand mature in His teachings and fully formed in the likeness of the Anointed, our Liberating King.*
> —Ephesians 4:13 VOICE

God's Word Speaking to Me

The ultimate goal of every Christian is to look like Jesus, but to get there, we better have a clear picture of who Jesus really is. Take a look at these scriptures describing Him and journal who He is to you.

John 14:6 ❀ 1 Timothy 2:5 ❀ John 3:16 ❀ John 1:1 ❀ Acts 4:11-12 ❀ John 1:14 ❀ Hebrews 13:8 ❀ John 8:58 ❀ Isaiah 53:4-5 ❀ Hebrews 2:14 ❀ Colossians 2:9 ❀ Philippians 2:8-11 ❀ 1 Corinthians 15:3-4 ❀ Isaiah 9:6 ❀ Hebrews 4:3 ❀ Romans 10:9 ❀ Hebrews 12:2 ❀ 1 Peter 2:24 ❀ Matthew 16:15-16 ❀ Revelation 22:13 ❀ Matthew 28:18 ❀ 2 Corinthians 5:21 ❀ Revelation 1:5 ❀ Colossians 1:17 ❀ Galatians 2:20 ❀ Matthew 24:44

My Prayer

My Praise Report

Bearing Fruit

You must go on growing in me and I will grow in you. For just as the branch cannot bear any fruit unless it shares the life of the vine, so you can produce nothing unless you go on growing in me. I am the vine itself, you are the branches. It is the man who shares my life and whose life I share who proves fruitful.
—JOHN 15:2-5 PHILLIPS

But the fruit produced by the Holy Spirit within you is divine love in all its varied expressions: joy that overflows, peace that subdues, patience that endures, kindness in action, a life full of virtue, faith that prevails, gentleness of heart, and strength of spirit. Never set the law above these qualities, for they are meant to be limitless.
—GALATIANS 5:22-23 TPT

God's Word Speaking to Me

Look up these scriptures and journal what they mean to you as you are ever growing in Him and bearing fruit!

John 15:16 ❖ Galatians 2:20 ❖ Philippians 1:11 ❖ Matthew 13:23 ❖ Philippians 4:17 ❖ Psalm 1:3 ❖ Galatians 5:22-24 ❖ Colossians 1:9-10 ❖ John 12:24 ❖ John 15:2-5

Reflection

Tending to the Garden

You will bear more fruit and better fruit in your spiritual life if you do a little gardening. So take a few minutes to make a note of any "weeds" that need pulling in your garden. Remember—this is *your* journal for your eyes only!

My Prayer

My Praise Report

Patience

…Is your life full of difficulties and temptations? Then be happy, for when the way is rough, your patience has a chance to grow. So let it grow, and don't try to squirm out of your problems. For when your patience is finally in full bloom, then you will be ready for anything, strong in character, full and complete.
—JAMES 1:2-4 TLB

God's Word Speaking to Me

As you *patiently* pore over each scripture below, you will come away with new insight on the necessity and power of patience. Jot down how each scripture applies to your life!

Proverbs 14:29

....

....

....

....

Romans 8:25

....

....

Galatians 6:9

Romans 12:12

Hebrews 10:36

Luke 21:19

Psalm 27:14

Exodus 14:14

Romans 5:2-4

My Prayer

My Praise Report

Humility

...God goes against the willful proud;
God gives grace to the willing humble.
—JAMES 4:6 MSG

Get down on your knees before the Mas-
ter; it's the only way you'll get on your feet.
—JAMES 4:10 MSG

My Prayer

Before you pray, take a minute to read through this prayer and note the scriptures used in writing it! It will drive home how important it is to pray according to God's Word, which we covered in Building Block #3 in "How to Build Prayers That Avail Much."

Dear Father, I wrap around myself the apron of a humble servant, for You resist the proud but multiply grace and favor to the humble. I renounce pride and arrogance, and I choose to humble myself under Your mighty hand, that in due time You may exalt me.
I humble myself and submit to Your Word that speaks (exposes, sifts, analyzes, and judges) the very thoughts and purposes of my heart. I test my own actions so that I might have appropriate self-esteem, without comparing myself to anyone else. The security of Your

guidance will allow me to carry my own load with energy and confidence.

I hide Your Word in my heart. As one of Your chosen people, I clothe myself with compassion, kindness, humility, gentleness, and patience. I bear with others and forgive whatever grievances I may have against anyone. I forgive as You forgave me. And over all these virtues I put on love, which binds them all together in perfect unity. I let the peace of Christ rule in my heart, and I am thankful for Your grace and the power of the Holy Spirit. I incline my ear to wisdom and apply my heart to understanding and insight. I wait before You in expectation. I listen carefully and make note as You speak to my heart. I pray in Jesus' name. Amen.

God's Word Speaking to Me

1 Peter 5:5-7 TPT, AMPC ❀ Proverbs 22:4 NIV ❀ Proverbs 3:7-8 NIV ❀ Psalm 119:11 ❀ Hebrews 4:12 AMPC ❀ Colossians 3:12-15 NIV ❀ Galatians 6:4-5 NIV ❀ Matthew 6:10 NIV ❀ Proverbs 2:2 NIV

Practicing Humility

Take a minute to list action steps that will put humility to work in your life!

My Praise Report

Fearless

Don't be afraid. Just trust me.
—Mark 5:36 TLB

For God hath not given us the spirit of fear;
but of power, and of love, and of a sound mind.
—2 Timothy 1:7 NKJV

God's Word Speaking to Me

If God has not given you a spirit of fear, that means fear in your life comes from the devil, man, or yourself. Even then, you don't have to put up with it! Check out the scriptures below. And make notes!

Psalm 56:3-4 TLB

....

....

....

....

....

2 Timothy 1:7-8 TPT

....

....

John 14:1,17 TLB

Romans 8:15 NASB

Psalm 27:1-3 TLB, MSG

My Prayer

My Praise Report

Faithfulness

Do not slack in your faithfulness and hard work. Let your spirit be on fire, bubbling up and boiling over, as you serve the Lord.
—ROMANS 12:11 VOICE

God's Word Speaking to Me

God is faithful and true, and He expects you to be as well. Write out each scripture below in your favorite Bible version and focus on what God is saying to you!

1 Corinthians 4:2

Galatians 5:22

Matthew 25:21

....
....
....
....
....

Proverbs 28:20

....
....
....
....
....

Deuteronomy 7:9

....
....
....
....

Psalm 36:5

....
....

Psalm 101:6

Reflection

Checkup Time!

Assess your faithfulness! Remember, this journal is between you and God.

My Prayer

My Praise Report

No Longer Intimidated

*For the Holy Spirit, God's gift, does not want you
to be afraid of people, but to be wise and strong,
and to love them and enjoy being with them.*
—2 Timothy 1:7 TLB

*Don't be afraid of people. I am with you,
and I will rescue you, declares the Lord.*
—Jeremiah 1:8 GW

Reflection

Don't Buy into It!

Intimidation has its roots in fear, and God has not given
you a spirit of fear (2 Tim. 1:7), so just plain don't buy into it.

What intimidates you? Once you label it, you and
God's Word will team up to eliminate it. Be honest! This is
your journal.

God's Word Speaking to Me

What does God have to say about those things that intimate you? List five scriptures that speak to each or a whole lot more below!

1. _____

2. _____

3. _____

4. _____

5. _____

Reflection

Psalm 118:6-16 MSG

Pushed to the wall, I called to God; from the wide open spaces, he answered. God's now at my side and I'm not afraid; who would dare lay a hand on me? God's my strong champion; I flick off my enemies like flies. Far better to take refuge in God than trust in people; Far better to take refuge in God than trust in celebrities. Hemmed in by barbarians, in God's name I rubbed their faces in the dirt; Hemmed in and with no way out, in God's name I rubbed their faces in the dirt; Like swarming bees, like wild prairie fire, they hemmed me in; in God's name I rubbed their faces in the dirt. I was right on the cliff-edge, ready to fall, when God grabbed and held me. God's my strength, he's also my song, and now he's my salvation.Hear the shouts, hear the triumph songs in the camp of the saved?"The hand of God has turned the tide!The hand of God is raised in victory!The hand of God has turned the tide!"

Psalm 56:11 TLB

I am trusting God—oh, praise his promises! I am not afraid of anything mere man can do to me! Yes, praise his promises.

My Prayer

My Praise Report

A Discerning Heart

For the Word that God speaks is alive and full of power [making it active, operative, energizing, and effective]; it is sharper than any two-edged sword, penetrating to the dividing line of the breath of life (soul) *and [the immortal] spirit, and of joints and marrow [of the deepest parts of our nature], exposing and sifting and analyzing and judging the very thoughts and purposes of the heart.*
Hebrews 4:12 AMPC

God's Word Speaking to Me

Paul's Prayers

The apostle Paul wrote and prayed the following prayers that changed my life. They will change yours too. Pray them faithfully aloud over yourself, your loved ones, and anyone else who needs to walk in light and truth. Be sure to personalize these prayers with your name or another's!

Ephesians 1:16-21 AMPC

"I do not cease to give thanks for you, making mention of you in my prayers. [For I always pray to] the God of our Lord Jesus Christ, the Father of glory, that He may grant you a spirit of wisdom and revelation [of insight into mysteries and secrets] in the [deep and intimate] knowledge of Him, By

having the eyes of your heart flooded with light, so that you can know and understand the hope to which He has called you, and how rich is His glorious inheritance in the saints (His set-apart ones), *And [so that you can know and understand] what is the immeasurable and unlimited and surpassing greatness of His power in and for us who believe, as demonstrated in the working of His mighty strength, Which He exerted in Christ when He raised Him from the dead and seated Him at His [own] right hand in the heavenly [places], Far above all rule and authority and power and dominion and every name that is named [above every title that can be conferred], not only in this age and in this world, but also in the age and the world which are to come."*

Ephesians 3:14-21 AMPC

"I bow my knees before the Father of our Lord Jesus Christ, For Whom every family in heaven and on earth is named [that Father from Whom all fatherhood takes its title and derives its name]. May He grant you out of the rich treasury of His glory to be strengthened and reinforced with mighty power in the inner man by the [Holy] Spirit [Himself indwelling your innermost being and personality]. May Christ through your faith [actually] dwell (settle down, abide, make His permanent home) *in your hearts! May you be rooted deep in love and founded securely on love, That you may have the power and be strong to apprehend and grasp with all the saints [God's devoted people, the experience of that love] what is the breadth and length and height and depth [of it]; [That you may really come] to know [practically, through experience for yourselves] the love of Christ, which far surpasses mere knowledge [without experience]; that you may be filled [through all your being] unto all the fullness of God [may have the richest measure of the divine Presence, and become a body wholly filled and flooded with God Himself]! Now to Him*

Who, by (in consequence of) *the [action of His] power that is at work within us, is able to [carry out His purpose and] do superabundantly, far over and above all that we [dare] ask or think [infinitely beyond our highest prayers, desires, thoughts, hopes, or dreams]—To Him be glory in the church and in Christ Jesus throughout all generations forever and ever. Amen* (so be it)."

Philippians 1:9-19 AMPC

"This I pray: that your love may abound yet more and more and extend to its fullest development in knowledge and all keen insight [that your love may

display itself in greater depth of acquaintance and more comprehensive discernment], So that you may surely learn to sense what is vital, and approve and prize what is excellent and of real value [recognizing the highest and the best, and distinguishing the moral differences], and that you may be untainted and pure and unerring and blameless [so that with hearts sincere and certain and unsullied, you may approach] the day of Christ [not stumbling nor causing others to stumble]. May you abound in and be filled with the fruits of righteousness (of right standing with God and right doing) which come through Jesus Christ (the Anointed One), to the honor and praise of God [[b]that His glory may be both manifested and recognized]. Now I want you to know and continue to rest assured, brethren, that what [has happened] to me [this imprisonment] has actually only served to advance and give a renewed impetus to the [spreading of the] good news (the Gospel). So much is this a fact that throughout the whole imperial guard and to all the rest [here] my imprisonment has become generally known to be in Christ [that I am a prisoner in His service and for Him]. And [also] most of the brethren have derived fresh confidence in the Lord because of my chains and are much more bold to speak and publish fearlessly the Word of God [acting with more freedom and indifference to the consequences]. Some, it is true, [actually] preach Christ (the Messiah) [for no better reason than] out of envy and rivalry (party spirit), but others are doing so out of a loyal spirit and goodwill. The latter [proclaim Christ] out of love, because they recognize and know that I am [providentially] put here for the defense of the good news (the Gospel). But the former preach Christ out of a party spirit, insincerely [out of no pure motive, but thinking to annoy me], supposing they are making my bondage more bitter and my chains more galling. But what does it matter, so long as either way, whether in pretense [for personal ends] or in all honesty [for the furtherance of the Truth], Christ is being proclaimed? And in that I [now] rejoice, yes, and I shall rejoice [hereafter] also. For I am well assured and indeed know that through your prayers and a bountiful supply of the Spirit of Jesus Christ (the Messiah) this will turn out for my preservation (for the spiritual health and [f]welfare of my own soul) and avail toward the saving work of the Gospel."

My Praise Report

Create Your Own Prayer

In what area do you want to grow?

....

....

....

....

....

....

....

....

God's Word Speaking to Me

....

....

....

....

....

....

My Prayer

My Praise Report

Create Your Own Prayer

In what area do you want to grow?

_____

_____

_____

_____

_____

_____

_____

_____

_____

_____

God's Word Speaking to Me

_____

_____

_____

_____

_____

_____

_____

My Prayer

....
....
....
....
....
....
....
....
....
....
....
....
....
....

My Praise Report

....
....
....
....

Create Your Own Prayer

In what area do you want to grow?

_____
_____
_____
_____
_____
_____
_____
_____

God's Word Speaking to Me

_____
_____
_____
_____
_____
_____
_____

My Prayer

My Praise Report

Create Your Own Prayer

In what area do you want to grow?

....
....
....
....
....
....
....
....

God's Word Speaking to Me

....
....
....
....
....
....
....

My Prayer

....
....
....
....
....
....
....
....
....
....
....
....
....
....
....
....

My Praise Report

....
....
....
....

Create Your Own Prayer

In what area do you want to grow?

_____

_____

_____

_____

_____

_____

_____

_____

God's Word Speaking to Me

_____

_____

_____

_____

_____

_____

_____

My Prayer

My Praise Report

Create Your Own Prayer

In what area do you want to grow?

God's Word Speaking to Me

My Prayer

....

....

....

....

....

....

....

....

....

....

....

....

....

....

....

....

My Praise Report

....

....

....

....

....

Create Your Own Prayer

In what area do you want to grow?

....

God's Word Speaking to Me

....

My Prayer

....
....
....
....
....
....
....
....
....
....
....
....
....
....
....

My Praise Report

....
....
....
....

Prayers for My Personal Needs

Finding God's Direction

For all who are led by the Spirit
of God are children of God.
—ROMANS 8:14 NLT

Do not be conformed to this world, but
be transformed by the renewing of your
mind, that you may prove what is that
good and acceptable and perfect will of God.
—ROMANS 12:2 NKJV

My Prayer

Father, Thank You for instructing me in the way I
should go. Thank You for guiding me and leading me
into Your plans and purposes for my life. My steps are
ordered by You, and Your Word is a lamp to my feet and
a light to my path.

Psalm 37:23   Psalm 119:105

My path is growing brighter and brighter until it
reaches the full light of day.

Proverbs 4:18

Jesus was made unto me wisdom. Confusion is not a
part of my life. I am not confused about

1 Corinthians 14:33

Your will for my life. I trust in You and lean not unto my own understanding. As I acknowledge You in

Proverbs 3:5-6

all of my ways, You are directing my paths. I pray that I'm flooded with light and filled with the spirit

Ephesians 1:17-19

of wisdom and revelation in the knowledge of you. The Spirit of God shows me things to come.

John 16:13

I am a sheep who knows Your voice!

John 10:27

In Jesus' name, I pray. Amen.

God's Word Speaking to Me

Hebrews 4:12 AMPC says, *"For the Word that God speaks is alive and full of power [making it active, operative, energizing, and effective]; it is sharper than any two-edged sword, penetrating to the dividing line of the breath of life (soul) and [the immortal] spirit, and of joints and marrow [of the deepest parts of our nature], exposing and sifting and analyzing and judging the very thoughts and purposes of the heart."* So, as you meditate on the scriptures below, God's Word will help make God's will clear to you!

Romans 8:14 ❂ Psalm 32:8 TLB ❂ Romans 12:2 TPT ❂
John 10:3-4 ❂ Psalm 23:3 ❂ Proverbs 3:5-6 ❂ Proverbs 4:18 ❂
Psalm 16:11 ❂ Romans 12:2 ❂ Romans 8:14 ❂ Psalm 11:105 ❂
James 1:5 ❂ Proverbs 11:3 ❂ Proverbs 11:14 ❂ Proverbs 14:15

❀ Proverbs 15:22 ❀ Proverbs 16:9 ❀ Proverbs 19:21❀ Psalm 37:23 ❀ Jeremiah 29:11

....
....
....
....
....
....
....
....
....
....
....

My Praise Report

....
....
....
....
....
....
....

Healing and Health

...the blows that fell to him
have brought us healing.
—Isaiah 53:5 Moffatt

God's Word Speaking to Me

Take Your Medicine

Psalm 107:20 says, *"He sent his word, and healed them, and delivered them from their destructions."* How do we receive from the Word? Proverbs 4:20-22 (NLT) says: *"My child, pay attention to what I say. Listen carefully to my words. Don't lose sight of them. Let them penetrate deep into your heart, for they bring life to those who find them, and healing to their whole body."* The Hebrew word for *health* in verse 22 is "medicine." Take your healing medicine as you meditate on the following healing scriptures. And be sure to jot down what the Holy Spirit specifically speaks to your heart.

Isaiah 53:4-5 ❀ Exodus 15:25-26 ❀ Exodus 23:25 ❀ Psalm 103:2-3 ❀ Proverbs 17:22 ❀ Matthew 8:16-17 ❀ Luke 10:19 ❀ Galatians 3:13 ❀ Ephesians 4:27 ❀ 1 Peter 2:24 ❀ 3 John 2

....

....

....

....

....

Reflection

During Jesus' earthly ministry, He often ministered to crowds of people who needed healing and healed them all, but there were also 19 individual cases where Jesus ministered one on one. Let me challenge you to read through these Gospel accounts.

Three of the cases are listed below. As you meditate on them, Jesus—who is the same yesterday, today and forever—will bring healing to you!

- Matthew 8:1-4—Jesus healed the leper.
- Mark 5:25-34—Jesus healed the woman with the issue of blood.
- Matthew 8:5-13—Jesus spoke the "word only" to heal the Centurion's servant

....

....

....

....

My Prayer

....
....
....
....
....
....
....
....
....
....
....
....

My Praise Report

....
....
....
....
....
....

Financial Need

> *...You can be sure that God will take care of everything you need, his generosity exceeding even yours in the glory that pours from Jesus.*
> —Philippians 4:19-20 MSG

God's Word Speaking to Me

Let's take a look at these scriptures one by one that talk about God meeting your financial needs. Be sure to note how the Holy Spirit personalizes each scripture to you!

Psalm 56:1

Deuteronomy 8:18-19

Philippians 4:19

2 Corinthians 9:8 AMPC

Malachi 3:8-12

....

....

....

....

....

....

James 1:22-23 TPT

....

....

....

....

....

....

3 John 2

....

....

....

....

....

....

Reflection

Your Lions and Your Bears

When David was preparing to fight Goliath, he reminded himself of previous victories. First Samuel 17: 34-37 says, "When a lion or a bear comes to steal a lamb from the flock, I go after it with a club and rescue the lamb from its mouth. If the animal turns on me, I catch it by the jaw and club it to death. I have done this to both lions and bears, and I'll do it to this pagan Philistine, too, for he has defied the armies of the living God! The Lord who rescued me from the claws of the lion and the bear will rescue me from this Philistine!" (NLT).

Encourage yourself the same way! Before you pray asking God to meet your financial need, encourage yourself by recalling your past faith victories. List your "lions and bears" below!

1. _____

2. _____

3. _____

4. _____

5. _____

6. _____

7. _____

8. _____

My Prayer

I'll start, and you finish!

> *Father, I come to You concerning my financial situation. You are a very present help in trouble, and You are more than enough. Your Word declares that You shall supply all my need according to Your riches in glory by Christ Jesus. More specifically, Father, I pray...*

My Praise Report

Protection

*…God will be right there with
you; he'll keep you safe and sound.*
—Proverbs 3:26 MSG

The God-born are also the God-protected.
—1 John 5:18 MSG

My Prayer

I'll start, and you finish!

*Dear Father, thank You that You are my refuge and
my fortress. No evil shall befall me—no accident shall
overtake me—nor any plague or calamity come near
my home. You give Your angels special charge over
me to accompany and defend and preserve me in all
my ways. They are encamped around about me. You
are my Confidence, firm and strong. You keep my
foot from being caught in a trap or hidden danger.
Father, You give me safety and ease me—Jesus You are
my safety!*

Father, I also pray…

God's Word Speaking to Me

Proverbs 3:23 AMPC ❖ Psalm 91 AMPC ❖ Psalm 112:7 ❖ Psalm 34:7, 19 ❖ Psalm 3:5 ❖ Proverbs 3:23-26 ❖ Psalm 4:8 AMPC ❖ Isaiah 49:25 ❖ Psalm 121:1-8 MSG ❖ 1 Peter 1:18-19 ❖ 1 John 5:18-19 MSG ❖ Psalm 118:6-9 TPT, ESV ❖ Psalm 56:11 ❖ 2 Thessalonians 3:3 ❖ Deuteronomy 31:6 ❖ Isaiah 41:10 ❖ Psalm 46:1 ❖ 2 Samuel 22:3-4 ❖ Psalm 23 ❖ Romans 8:38-39 MSG, TLB, TPT

....

....

....

....

....

....

....

....

....

Reflection

The Christian's Assurance Policy

Psalm 91 MSG

> *You who sit down in the High God's presence, spend the night in Shaddai's shadow, Say this: "God, you're my refuge. I trust in you and I'm safe!" That's right—he rescues you from hidden traps, shields you from deadly hazards. His huge outstretched arms protect you— under them you're perfectly safe; his arms fend off all harm. Fear nothing—not wild wolves in the night, not flying arrows in the day, Not disease that prowls through the darkness, not disaster that erupts at high noon. Even though others succumb all around, drop like flies right and left, no*

harm will even graze you. You'll stand untouched, watch it all from a distance, watch the wicked turn into corpses. Yes, because God's your refuge, the High God your very own home, Evil can't get close to you, harm can't get through the door. He ordered his angels to guard you wherever you go. If you stumble, they'll catch you; their job is to keep you from falling. You'll walk unharmed among lions and snakes, and kick young lions and serpents from the path. If you'll hold on to me for dear life," says God, "I'll get you out of any trouble. I'll give you the best of care if you'll only get to know and trust me. Call me and I'll answer, be at your side in bad times; I'll rescue you, then throw you a party. I'll give you a long life, give you a long drink of salvation!

My Praise Report

Peace

> *You will keep him in perfect peace, whose*
> *mind is stayed on You, because he trusts in You.*
> Isaiah 26:3 NLT

God's Word Speaking to Me

Philippians 4:6-7 MSG ❖ Colossians 3:15 AMPC ❖ Proverbs
16:7 NLT ❖ Psalm 34:14 MSG, TPT, AMPC, NLT ❖ John
14:27 NLT, TPT, AMPC ❖ Isaiah 26:3 AMPC

My Prayer

Before you pray, track the scriptures used in this prayer. It
will build your faith to pray! Then finish the prayer with
your specific petitions.

> *Dear Father, I turn my back on worry. I embrace*
> *peace and refuse to let it get away! I make peace my*

life motto! I crave peace and choose peace in my life. I go after it, and I work to maintain it! When my life pleases you, Father, You make even my enemies to be at peace with me.

Lord, You said, "I leave the gift of peace with you— My peace. Not the kind of fragile peace given by the world, but My perfect peace…." I will not let my heart be troubled and afraid. I refuse to be agitated and disturbed. I will give all my worries and cares to You because You care for me. That means You care for me and love me, but it also means that You will do the caring—or thinking—for me!

Father, I will let petitions and praises shape my worries into prayers, and I will thank You for the answers. Your peace will keep my thoughts and heart quiet and at rest as I trust in Christ Jesus, my Lord. It is wonderful what happens when Jesus displaces worry at the center of my life.

Father, I also pray…

Reflection

Forewarned Is Forearmed

You've prayed and made peace your life motto as Psalm 34:14 TPT says! But list the enemies here below that often try to challenge your peace. Then answer each enemy with a scripture that will still the avenger and safeguard your peace.

1. _____

2. _____

3. _____

4. _____

5. _____

6. _____

7. _____

My Praise Report

Marital Bliss

Let marriage be held in honor among all…
—Hebrews 13:4 ESV

*A house is built by wisdom and
becomes strong through good sense.*
—Proverbs 24:3 NLT

Steadfast love and faithfulness meet; righteousness and peace kiss each other.
—Psalm 85:10 ESV

God's Word Speaking to Me

Two Are Better Than One

Marriage was God's idea from the very beginning. He told Adam that a man shall leave his father and mother and cleave to his wife, the two becoming one flesh. Two are better than one—as long as the two get along.

If you're married, let's do a little checkup. Candidly judge yourself in light of the scriptures below. If you come up short in an area, add God's Word to the mix. Ecclesiastes 4:12 (NLT) says, "…A triple-braided cord is not easily broken."

Ephesians 5:15-34 (whole chapter excellent) ◦ 1 Peter 4:8 ◦ 1 Peter 3:1-5 ◦ Colossians 3:18-19 ◦ Ephesians 4:32 ◦ Joshua 24:15

Reflection

God's Yardstick for Life and Marriage

1 Corinthians 13:1-7 MSG

If I speak with human eloquence and angelic ecstasy but don't love, I'm nothing but the creaking of a rusty gate. If I speak God's Word with power, revealing all his mysteries and making everything plain as day, and if I have faith that says to a mountain, "Jump," and it jumps, but I don't love, I'm nothing. If I give everything I own to the poor and even go to the stake to be burned as a martyr, but I don't love, I've gotten nowhere. So, no matter what I say, what I believe, and what I do, I'm bankrupt without love. Love never gives up. Love cares more for others than for self. Love doesn't want what it doesn't have. Love doesn't strut, Doesn't have a swelled head, Doesn't force itself on others, Isn't always "me first," Doesn't fly off the handle, Doesn't keep score of the sins of others, Doesn't revel when others grovel, Takes pleasure in the flowering of truth, Puts up with anything, Trusts God always, Always looks for the best, Never looks back, But keeps going to the end.

My Prayer

....
....
....
....
....
....
....
....
....
....
....
....
....

My Praise Report

....
....
....
....
....

New Friends

Friends come and friends go, but a true friend sticks by you like family.
—Proverbs 18:24 MSG

My Prayer

Father, help me to meet new friends and develop good friendships that are divine connections ordained by you. As iron sharpens iron, so friends sharpen the minds of each other so together we may find a worthy purpose in our relationship. Keep me well-balanced in my friendships so that I will always please You rather than pleasing other people.

Thank You for quality friends who help me build stronger character and draw me closer to You. Help me be a friend to others and love my friends at all times. I will laugh with those who laugh, I will rejoice with those who rejoice, and I will weep with those who weep. Teach me to be a quality friend. Your Word says that two are better than one, because if one falls, there will be someone to lift up that person. Instruct my heart and mold my character that I may be trustworthy over the friendships You are sending into my life.

Father, Your Word says bad friendships corrupt good morals, so thank You for the discernment to recognize healthy relationships and the courage to let go of detrimental friendships.

Jesus is my best Friend, and He sticks closer than a brother. I want to be that kind of friend to others. Thank You, Lord, that I can entrust myself and my need for friends into Your keeping. In the name of Jesus. Amen.

God's Word Speaking to Me

Proverbs 13:20 NIV ❊ 1 Corinthians 15:33 AMPC ❊ Ephesians 5:30 NIV ❊ Proverbs 27:17 CEV ❊ James 1:17 NIV ❊ Philippians 2:2-3 NIV ❊ Proverbs 17:17 ❊ Proverbs 13:20 NIV ❊ Romans 12:15-16 ❊ Psalm 84:11 NIV ❊ Proverbs 18:24 NKJV ❊ Ecclesiastes 4:9-10 NIV ❊ Psalm 37:4-5 NIV

Reflection

The Friend for Me is the Kind of Friend I Will Be

List the characteristics important to you to find in a friend—and realize that's the kind of friend God will expect you to be to others!

1. _____

2. _____

3. _____

4. _____

5. _____

6. _____

7. _____

8. _____

My Praise Report

Harmony in My Family

Live in harmony with one another....
—ROMANS 12:16 NIV

Friends love through all kinds of weather, and
families stick together in all kinds of trouble.
—PROVERBS 17:17 MSG

God's Word Speaking to Me

Romans 5:5 TPT ❖ Ephesians 4:32 ❖ Philippians 1:9 ❖ Isaiah 32:17 ❖ Colossians 3:14 ❖ Colossians 1:10, 12-14 TPT ❖ 1 Corinthians 13 ❖ Colossians 3:15 AMPC ❖ Romans 6:4 ❖ Ephesians 5:15-16 TPT ❖ Galatians 5:22 ❖ Hebrews 12:14 ❖ 1 Peter 3:11 ❖ 1 Thessalonians 5:15 ❖ James 3:18 ❖ Proverbs 3:1-35 ❖ John 3:16 TPT ❖ James 3:17-18 MSG

Reflection

What issues have challenged your family's peace, and what does God's Word say about them?

1. _____

2. _____

3. _____

4. _____

5. _____

6. _____

7. _____

My Prayer

I'll start, and you finish!

Dear Father, I purpose to walk in newness of life. The past will no longer define my relationships with my family. In the name of Jesus, I bind our emotions to the control of the Holy Spirit who lives in us. I bind our spirits, souls, and bodies to the peace that acts as an umpire in our hearts. The peace of God will decide and settle with finality all questions that arise in our minds. I loose from each of us those past grievances and wrong attitudes toward others. Our love for one another is patient and kind. Your love that cascades into our hearts drives fear of rejection and ridicule out of doors. Thank You for making each of us unique and giving us the courage to be the people You created us to be. May we speak the truth in love to one another. Dear Father…

Action

Ask the Holy Spirit for practical ways to enact harmony in your family and list them here!

1. _____
2. _____
3. _____
4. _____
5. _____
6. _____
7. _____
8. _____
9. _____

My Praise Report

Carefree

Live carefree before God;
he is most careful with you.
—1 PETER 5:6-7 MSG

Those who enter into Christ's being-
here-for-us no longer have to live under
a continuous, low-lying black cloud.
—ROMANS 8:2 MSG

God's Word Speaking to Me

Colossians 1:13 ❀ Hebrews 12:1-3 MSG ❀ Romans 8:2 ❀
2 Timothy 1:12 ❀ 1 Peter 5:6-7 AMPC ❀ Philippians 4:6-9
TPT, MSG ❀ Psalm 55:22 ❀ John 14:1 ❀ Psalm 138:8 ❀
James 1:22-25 ❀ 2 Corinthians 10:5

Action

Cares That Try to Steal My Peace

Write down these cares and face them squarely. Then boldly declare God's Word over them.

....

....

....

....

....

Reflection

The Think Test

If the thoughts running through your mind pass the test below, you can think about them. If not, kick them out in Jesus' name!

> *Summing it all up, friends, I'd say you'll do best by filling your minds and meditating on things* **true, noble, reputable, authentic, compelling, gracious**—*the* **best, not the worst; the beautiful, not the ugly; things to praise, not things to curse** (Philippians 4:8 MSG)

> *Fix your thoughts on what is* **true,** *and* **honorable,** *and* **right,** *and* **pure,** *and* **lovely,** *and* **admirable.** *Think about* **things that are excellent and worthy of praise** (Philippians 4:8 NLT).

My Prayer

Father, thank You that I have been delivered from the power of darkness and translated into the Kingdom of Your dear Son. I commit to live free from worry in the name of Jesus, for the law of the Spirit of life in Christ Jesus has made me free from the law of sin and death.

I cast the whole of my cares—all my anxieties, all my worries, all my concerns—once and for all on You. You care for me affectionately and care about me watchfully. You sustain me.

I cast down imaginations, reasonings, and every high thing that exalts itself against the knowledge of You, and I bring into captivity every thought to the obedience of Christ. I lay aside every weight and the sin of worry, which so easily tries to ensnare me. I run with patience the race that is set before me, looking unto Jesus, the Author and Finisher of my faith. I start running—and never quit! When I find myself flagging in my faith, I keep my eyes on Jesus and study how He did it. That shoots adrenaline into my soul!

I will not let my heart be troubled. Instead, I abide in Your Word, and Your Word abides in me. Therefore, Father, I do not forget what manner of person I am. I look into the perfect law of liberty and continue therein, being not a forgetful hearer, but a doer of the Word and, thus, blessed in my doing!

Father, I am carefree—walking in that peace that passes all understanding. In Jesus' name. Amen.

Reflection

God's Promise to You

> ...*For He [God] Himself has said, I will not in any way fail you nor give you up nor leave you without support. [I will] not, [I will] not, [I will] not in any degree leave you helpless nor forsake nor let [you] down (relax My hold on you)! [Assuredly not!]* (Hebrews 13:5 AMPC).

My Praise Report

Watching My Words

*A word out of your mouth may seem
of no account, but it can accom-
plish nearly anything—or destroy it!*
—James 3:5 MSG

God's Word Speaking to Me

Ephesians 5:4 MSG, TPT ❖ Ephesians 4:27-32 MSG, TPT ❖ Proverbs 21:23 ❖ 2 Timothy 2:16 ❖ Proverbs 18:21 ❖ Ephesians 4:27 ❖ James 3:1-10 MSG ❖ James 1:6 ❖ Proverbs 8:6-7 ❖ John 6:63 ❖ 2 Corinthians 5:21 ❖ Colossians 3:16 ❖ Proverbs 4:23 ❖ Philemon 6

My Prayer

I'll start, and you finish!

Dear Father, today I make a commitment to guard my speech and watch the way I talk. I will forsake obscenities, worthless insults, and nonsensical words that bring disgrace and are unnecessary. I will lay aside ugly, hateful, and bitter words. I will lay aside words that don't agree with your Word, which is Your will. Instead. I will let my words become beautiful gifts that encourage others by speaking words of grace to help them. I will let worship fill my heart and spill out in my words. I will speak truth and life in every situation, for that is how You speak. I will...

Reflection

Replacing Bitter Words with Sweet Ones

If you've spoken hurtful or sharp words to someone, ask the Holy Spirit if you need to correct your words with an "I'm sorry" and soothing words to heal the wound.

My Praise Report

Victory in Jesus

Now the Son of God came to earth with the express purpose of liquidating the devil's activities.
—1 John 3:9 Phillips

How we thank God for all of this! It is he who makes us victorious through Jesus Christ our Lord!
—1 Corinthians 15:57 TLB

…In Christ, God leads us from place to place in one perpetual victory parade.
—2 Corinthians 2:14 MSG

God's Word Speaking to Me

1 John 3:1 MSG, NLT ❀ 1 John 4:15-18 TPT, NLT, AMPC ❀ Romans 8:31-39, TPT, MSG ❀ 1 John 4:4 ❀ Colossians 2:15 NLT ❀ Ephesians 2:4-7 ❀ 1 John 3:8 ❀ 2 Corinthians 2:14 NKJV ❀ 1 Corinthians 15:16 ❀ 1 Corinthians 15:57 TLB ❀ Isaiah 54:17

Reflection

Where's victory needed in your life? What does God's Word say about it?

....

....

....

....

....

....

....

....

My Prayer

I'll start, and you finish!

> *Father-God, what marvelous love You have extended to me! The light of Your love shined within me when You sent Your matchless Son into the world so that I might live through Him. I am Your child, and therefore, perfect love expels all fear. That means dread does not exist in my life, but full-grown (complete, perfect) love turns fear out of doors and expels every trace of terror! With You on my side, how can I lose? Greater are You in me than he that is in the world, and greater are You than this situation challenging me. You put every thing on the line for me, and there*

is nothing You would not gladly and freely do for me. Now, Father, I also pray...

My Praise Report

Passed the Past

Forget about what's happened;
don't keep going over old history.
—Isaiah 43:18-19 MSG

I've got my eye on the goal, where God is
beckoning us onward—to Jesus. I'm off
and running, and I'm not turning back.
—Philippians 3:14 MSG

God's Word Speaking to Me

Philippians 3:7-9 TLB ❀ Proverbs 3:5-6 NIV ❀ John 1:12 AMPC ❀ Philippians 3:10-11 NIV ❀ Psalm 32:5 AMPC ❀ Romans 6:4 ❀ Philippians 3:12-14 TLB, MSG ❀ Galatians 2:20 NIV, NKJV ❀ Isaiah 43:18-19 MSG, GNT ❀ 2 Corinthians 5:17 GNT ❀ Isaiah 43:25 ❀ Romans 8:1 ❀ Luke 9:62 ❀ 1 Corinthians 6:12 ESV ❀ John 14:1 ❀ Psalm 34:18 Voice ❀ Psalm 34:17-19 TPT ❀ Luke 4:18-19 TPT ❀ Psalm 32:5 AMPC ❀ 2 Corinthians 10:4-5 NKJV ❀ Isaiah 26:3

Action

Memories: Good, Bad, or Ugly

Do you have memories that bring you pain, guilt, shame, or fear? Lay them out here and now. Then tell those memories they are nothing but old history, and you've moved on in Jesus!

1. _____

2. _____

3. _____

4. _____

5. _____

6. _____

7. _____

Reflection

Isaiah 43:18-19 MSG

> *This is what God says, the God who builds a road right through the ocean, who carves a path through pounding waves, The God who summons horses and chariots and armies—they lie down and then can't get up; they're snuffed out like so many candles: "Forget about what's happened; don't keep going over old history. Be alert, be present. I'm about to do something brand-new. It's bursting out! Don't you*

see it? There it is! I'm making a road through the desert, rivers in the badlands. Wild animals will say 'Thank you!' —the coyotes and the buzzards— Because I provided water in the desert, rivers through the sunbaked earth, drinking water for the people I chose, the people I made especially for myself, a people custom-made to praise me.

My Prayer

I'll start, and you finish!

Dear Father, I unfold my past and put into proper perspective those things that are behind. I have been crucified with Christ, and I no longer live, but Christ lives in me. The life I live in the body, I live by faith in the Son of God, who loved me and gave Himself for me. I trust in You, Lord, with all my heart and lean not on my own under standing. In all my ways I acknowledge You, and You will make my paths straight. I cast down rebel thoughts that would steal my peace of mind. I will bring all my energies to bear on this one thing: Regardless of my past, I look forward to what lies ahead. I strain to reach the end of the race and receive the prize for which You are calling me up to heaven because of what Christ Jesus did for me. Father, I pray...

My Praise Report

Favor

…You will find favor and understand-
ing with both God and men— you will
gain the reputation of living life well.
—PROVERBS 3:4 TPT

God's Word Speaking to Me

Numbers 6:25 AMPC ❖ Psalm 8:5 ❖ Deuteronomy 28:13 ❖ Ephesians 2:10, 17 ❖ Matthew 6:33 ❖ Luke 2:40 ❖ Proverbs 11:27 ❖ Ephesians 6:24 ❖ Daniel 1:9, 17 AMPC ❖ Luke 6:38 ❖ Esther 2:15,17 ❖ Zechariah 12:10 AMPC ❖ Ephesians 3:19-20 ❖ Genesis 39:21 ❖ Exodus 3:21 ❖ Exodus 11:3 ❖ Deuteronomy 33:23 ❖ Joshua 11:20 ❖ 1 Samuel 16:22 ❖ Esther 2:17 ❖ Esther 5:8 ❖ Esther 8:5 ❖ Psalm 44:3 ❖ Proverbs 3:4

Reflection

List the benefits God's favor will bring to you!

1. _____
2. _____
3. _____
4. _____
5. _____
6. _____
7. _____
8. _____

My Prayer

My Praise Report

Sweet Sleep

> *Your mind will be clear, free from fear; when you lie down to rest, you will be refreshed by sweet sleep.*
> —PROVERBS 3:24 VOICE

> *The Lord will command His lovingkindness in the daytime, and in the night His song shall be with me—a prayer to the God of my life.*
> —PSALM 42:8 NKJV

God's Word Speaking to Me

Proverbs 3:24 VOICE, CEV ❀ Psalm 91:11 ❀ Psalm 34:7 ❀ 2 Corinthians 10:5 ❀ Psalm 103:20 NKJV ❀ Psalm 127:2 ❀ Psalm 4:8 ❀ Proverbs 6:10 ❀ Psalm 121:3-4 NLT, MSG ❀ Psalm 91:1-16 ❀ Matthew 8:24 ❀ Psalm 42:8 ❀ Proverbs 3:24 Voice ❀ Matthew 11:28-30 ❀ Jeremiah 31:26 ❀ Psalm 3:4-5 ❀ Proverbs 1:33 Voice

Reflection

Count Blessings—Not Sheep
Psalm 103:1-13 TPT

With my whole heart, with my whole life, and with my innermost being, I bow in wonder and love before you, the holy God! Yahweh, you are my soul's celebration. How could I ever forget the miracles of kindness you've done for me? You kissed my heart with forgiveness, in spite of all I've done. You've healed me inside and out from every disease. You've rescued me from hell and saved my life. You've crowned me with love and mercy. You satisfy my every desire with good things. You've supercharged my life so that I soar again like a flying eagle in the sky! You're a God who makes things right, giving justice to the defenseless. You unveiled to Moses your plans and showed Israel's sons what you could do. Lord, you're so kind and tenderhearted and so patient with people who fail you! Your love is like a flooding river overflowing its banks with kindness. You don't look at us only to find our faults, just so that you can hold a grudge against us. You may discipline us for our many sins, but never as much as we really deserve. Nor do you get even with us for what we've done. Higher than the highest heavens— that's how high your tender mercy extends! Greater than the grandeur of heaven above is the greatness of your loyal love, towering over all who fear you and bow down before you! Farther than from a sunrise to a sunset—that's how far you've removed our guilt from us. The same way a loving father feels toward his children—that's but a sample of your tender feelings toward us, your beloved children, who live in awe of you.

My Prayer

Father, I bring every thought, every imagination, and every dream into the captivity and obedience of Jesus Christ right now in Jesus' name. My mind—awake or asleep—will be clear and free from fear. I will rest without worry and sleep soundly.

Thank You that even as I sleep, my heart counsels me and reveals to me Your purpose and plan. Thank You for sweet sleep, for You promised Your beloved sweet sleep. Therefore, my heart is glad, and my spirit rejoices. My body and soul rest and confidently dwell in safety. I will awake refreshed and ready for my day in Jesus' name. Amen.

Action

David counted blessings for us all in the beautiful psalm we just read, but now it's your turn! List the blessings God has showered upon you and your family as you prepare for the sweet sleep God's Word promises.

My Praise Report

Create Your Own Prayer

What need will you take to the Father in prayer?

....
....
....
....
....
....
....
....

God's Word Speaking to Me

....
....
....
....
....
....
....
....

My Prayer

My Praise Report

Create Your Own Prayer

What need will you take to the Father in prayer?

....

....

....

....

....

....

....

....

God's Word Speaking to Me

....

....

....

....

....

....

....

....

....

My Prayer

My Praise Report

Create Your Own Prayer

What need will you take to the Father in prayer?

....

....

....

....

....

....

....

....

God's Word Speaking to Me

....

....

....

....

....

....

....

....

My Prayer

....

....

....

....

....

....

....

....

....

....

....

....

....

....

My Praise Report

....

....

....

....

....

....

....

Create Your Own Prayer

What need will you take to the Father in prayer?

....
....
....
....
....
....
....
....

God's Word Speaking to Me

....
....
....
....
....
....
....
....

My Prayer

My Praise Report

Create Your Own Prayer

What need will you take to the Father in prayer?

....
....
....
....
....
....
....
....
....
....

God's Word Speaking to Me

....
....
....
....
....
....
....
....
....

My Prayer

My Praise Report

Create Your Own Prayer

What need will you take to the Father in prayer?

....
....
....
....
....
....
....
....

God's Word Speaking to Me

....
....
....
....
....
....
....
....
....

My Prayer

My Praise Report

Create Your Own Prayer

What need will you take to the Father in prayer?

God's Word Speaking to Me

My Prayer

My Praise Report

Prayers for Others

Someone Needing Salvation

My Prayer

Before you pray, take a minute to pinpoint the scriptures used in this prayer. It will bolster your faith to pray! Then insert the name of the person you're praying for in the blanks, and take your prayer to the throne room.

Father, I come before You to stand in the gap and pray for _____ who is lost and without You. I pray in agreement with Jesus who is able to save to the uttermost those who come to You through Him because He always lives to make intercession for them.

_____ mind is blinded by the god of this world, the devil. So I take a stand against these unseen spirits who have held this person in darkness and bondage and break the devil's power to blind his/her mind in Jesus' name. I pray _____ is delivered from the power of darkness and comes to the kingdom of the Son of Your love, in whom we have redemption through His blood, the forgiveness of sins. May Your brilliant light shine out of darkness and cascade into them that they might see the knowledge of grace and truth.

When the Light shines out of darkness, _____ will hear the Good News of the gospel. He/she will call upon the name of the Lord and be saved. He/she will receive Jesus and come out of the snare of the devil who has held them captive.

Thank You, Father, for sending laborers across _____ path with the truth. He/she shall open his/her eyes and turn from darkness to light— from the power of Satan to Jesus. In Jesus' name, amen.

God's Word Speaking to Me

Hebrews 7:25 NKJV ❋ 2 Corinthians 4:1-6 TPT ❋ 1 Corinthians 10:3-5 NLT ❋ Romans 15:21 AMPC ❋ Matthew 9:38 ❋ 2 Timothy 2:26 AMPC ❋ Colossians 1:13 NKJV ❋ 2 Peter 3:8-10 TPT ❋ Ephesians 1:17-19 AMPC ❋ Romans 10:9-10 ❋ Isaiah 54:13 ❋ Psalm 2:8

Action

A Declaration of Faith

I'll start, and you finish!

Through the eye of faith, I see _____
*born again and walking with Jesus all the days of his
or her life. And...*

. . . .

. . . .

. . . .

. . . .

. . . .

. . . .

. . . .

My Praise Report

. . . .

. . . .

. . . .

. . . .

My Friend Facing Trouble

God's a safe-house for the battered, a sanctuary during bad times. The moment you arrive, you relax; you're never sorry you knocked.
—Psalm 9:9 MSG

God, you're such a safe and powerful place to find refuge! You're a proven help in time of trouble— more than enough and always available whenever I need you.
—Psalm 46:1 TPT

God Word Speaking to Me

Before you pray for your friend, look up the following scriptures in the Bible versions suggested. Different wording often brings new insight to the scripture's meaning. And don't forget to journal a few notes!

Psalm 9:9 MSG, AMPC, NLT

Psalm 57:1-2 AMPC, MSG

Psalm 27:5-7 AMPC , MSG

Psalm 46:1 TPT, NLT

2 Corinthians 12:8-10 TPT

John 14:27 AMPC

Psalm 34:17-20 AMPC, MSG

Romans 5:3-5 AMPC

My Prayer

My Praise Report

My Child's Destiny

Children are a gift from the Lord....
—Psalm 127:3 TLB

*Start children off on the way they should go, and
even when they are old they will not turn from it.*
—Proverbs 22:6 NIV

God's Word Speaking to Me

Psalm 127:3 ❋ Isaiah 54:13 ❋ Luke 2:52 ❋ Psalm 119:99 ❋
Romans 12:2 ❋ Isaiah 55:11 ❋ Proverbs 3:4 ❋ Proverbs 22:6
❋ Ephesians 6:1-4 ❋ Colossians 3:20 ❋ Deuteronomy 6:7 ❋
Ephesians 4:27 ❋ Romans 12:11 VOICE ❋ Psalm 37:3 TPT
❋ Ephesians 2:10 TPT ❋ Matthew 18:18 ❋ 2 Corinthians 2:11
❋ John 14:13 ❋ 2 Timothy 2:26 ❋ Psalm 91:1,11 ❋ John 14:26 ❋
Deuteronomy 28:8,13 ❋ Romans 12:1-2 ❋ 3 John 2

Reflection

Deuteronomy 6:7-9

Take a look at Deuteronomy 6 in the three Bible versions below. These verses tell you how to build God's Word in your children so it will lead them to their destinies.

"Write these commandments that I've given you today on your hearts. Get them inside of you and then get them inside your children. Talk about them wherever you are, sitting at home or walking in the street; talk about them from the time you get up in the morning to when you fall into bed at night. Tie them on your hands and foreheads as a reminder; inscribe them on the doorposts of your homes and on your city gates" (MSG).

"You must teach them to your children and talk about them when you are at home or out for a walk; at bedtime and the first thing in the morning" (TLB).

"Repeat them to your children. Talk about them when you're sitting together in your home and when you're walking together down the road. Make them the last thing you talk about before you go to bed and the first thing you talk about the next morning (VOICE).

My Prayer

My Praise Report

My Teen on Track

He [God} will return parents' hearts to their children and children's hearts to their parents....
MALACHI 4:6 VOICE
Intelligent children listen to their parents; foolish children do their own thing.
PROVERBS 13:1 MSG
...Don't squander your precious life.
PROVERBS 8:32 MSG

God's Word Speaking to Me

Proverbs 8:6-7 ❋ 1 Peter 5:7 ❋ Proverbs 8:32 MSG ❋ Proverbs 22:6 MSG ❋ Psalm 37:4 ❋ Isaiah 1:19 ❋ John 14:6 ❋ Isaiah 54:13 ❋ Ephesians 6:1-3 ❋ 2 Corinthians 5:18-19 ❋ 1 John 1:9 ❋ Colossians 3:21 TLB, MSG ❋ Proverbs 15:31 TLB, GW ❋ Isaiah 61:1 ❋ John 16:13 ❋ Jeremiah 1:12 ❋ Proverbs 13:1 TLB ❋ Ephesians 4:31-32 ❋ Malachi 4:6 ❋ Psalm 37: 23 ❋ 2 Corinthians 4:4 ❋ Ephesians 1:16-21 AMPC ❋ Ephesians 2:10 AMPC ❋ Psalm 37: 5 Voice ❋ Romans 12:1-2 ❋ Philippians 1:9-19 AMPC ❋ Ephesians 3:14-21 AMPC

....

....

....

My Prayer

I'll start, and you finish!

Dear Father, I affirm Your Word over _____. *I commit my son/daughter to You and delight myself in You. Thank You for delivering him/her out of rebellion and into your perfect will for his/her life.* _____ *steps are ordered, and he/she will walk in your perfect will—the steps you've arranged for him/her to live the good life.*

The first commandment with a promise is to the child who obeys his/her parents in the Lord. You said that all will be well with him/her, and he/she will live long on the earth. I affirm this promise on behalf of my child, asking You to give _____ *an obedient spirit that he/she may honor, esteem, and value us as parents. He/she will not squander precious life! Father, forgive me for mistakes made out of my own unresolved hurts or selfishness, which may have caused hurt. I release the anointing that is upon Jesus to bind up and heal our broken hearts (mine and my son/daughter's). Give us the ability to understand*

and forgive one another, as God for Christ's sake has forgiven us. Thank You for the Holy Spirit who leads us into all truth.

Father, I also pray...

....
....
....
....
....
....
....
....
....
....
....

My Praise Report

....
....
....
....
....

Blessings for My Adult Children

*...[Taking paths which He prepared
ahead of time], that we should walk in
them [living the good life which He pre-
arranged and made ready for us to live].*
—EPHESIANS 2:10 AMPC

*May the Lord richly bless
both you and your children.*
—PSALM 115:14 TLB

God's Word Speaking to Me

Ephesians 2:10 AMPC ❖ Psalm 37:23 ❖ Isaiah 59:1 ❖ 3 John 2
❖ Philippians 4:19 ❖ Proverbs 3:4 ❖ Isaiah 58:8 ❖ 1 Peter 5:7
❖ Psalm 91 ❖ Joshua 24:15 ❖ Ephesians 1:15-23 AMPC ❖
Ephesians 3:14-21 AMPC ❖ Philippians 1:9-11 AMPC
Romans 5:5 ❖ Ephesians 4:31-32 ❖ Jeremiah 1:12 ❖ Jeremiah
29:11 ❖ Joshua 1:7-8 ❖ Deuteronomy 28:13 ❖ Deuteronomy
30:9 ❖ Genesis 39:3 NASB ❖ Psalm 115:14 ❖ 1 Kings 2:3
NIV ❖ Mark 10:9 ❖ Romans 12:1-2 ❖ Philippians 1:6

My Prayer

My Praise Report

My Government Leaders

First of all, I encourage you to make petitions, prayers, intercessions, and prayers of thanks for all people, for rulers, and for everyone who has authority over us. Pray for these people so that we can have a quiet and peaceful life always lived in a godly and reverent way. This is good and pleases God our Savior.
—1 TIMOTHY 2:1-3 GW

Blessed is the nation whose God is the Lord, The people He has chosen as His own inheritance.
—PSALM 33:12 NKJV

God's Word Speaking to Me

1 Timothy 2:1-3 ✳ 2 Chronicles 7:14 ✳ Proverbs 21:1-3 ✳ Proverbs 16:7 ✳ Proverbs 16:12 ✳ Proverbs 14:34 ✳ Psalm 33:12 ✳ Deuteronomy 28:10-11 ✳ Proverbs 2:10-12,21-22 ✳ Romans 8:37 ✳ Psalm 33:12 ✳ Psalm 9:9 ✳ Acts 12:24

My Prayer

Action

It's vital to pray, but it's also important to stand up for what's right and speak out for what's good. Here's how I'll give action to my prayers.

....

....

....

....

....

....

....

....

My Praise Report

....

....

....

....

....

....

....

....

My Pastor and My Church

I will give you shepherds after my own heart, who
will guide you with knowledge and understanding.
—Jeremiah 3:15 NLT

Now it's up to you. Be on your toes—both for
yourselves and your congregation of sheep. The
Holy Spirit has put you in charge of these people—
God's people they are—to guard and protect them.
God himself thought they were worth dying for.
—Acts 20:28 MSG

God's Word Speaking to Me

Isaiah 11:2-3 ❖ 2 Timothy 1:13-14 AMPC ❖ Isaiah 61:1,6
AMPC ❖ Ephesians 6:19-20 AMPC ❖ Isaiah 54:17 AMPC ❖
1 Peter 3:12 ❖ Ephesians 1:22-23 NKJV ❖ Hebrews 10:23-25
MSG ❖ Ephesians 4:15-16 MSG ❖ Ephesians 4:4-6 MSG ❖
Colossians 3:12-15 NKJV ❖ Ephesians 6:18-19 MSG ❖ 1 John
5:14-15 ❖ 1 Peter 3:8-9 NLT ❖ 1 Corinthians 1:10 AMPC
❖ John 17:22-23 NLT ❖ Matthew 18:19 AMPC ❖ Matthew
6:10 ❖ Ephesians 4:2-3 TPT ❖ Acts 4:24 ❖ Ephesians 4:11-
15 ❖ Romans 4:17 ❖ Philippians 4:19 ❖ 1 Corinthians 1:10 ❖
Romans 5:5 ❖ Acts 4:29 ❖ 1 Corinthians 3:9 ❖ Mark 16:20
❖ Psalm 63:4 ❖ Exodus 35:33 ❖ Matthew 25:37-50 CEV ❖
Matthew 28:18-20 TPT

....

My Prayer

I'll start, and you finish!

Dear Father-God, in the name of Jesus, I pray that the Spirit of the Lord will rest upon my pastor with wisdom, understanding, counsel, might, and knowledge. I ask you to make _____ of quick understanding because You, Lord, have anointed and qualified him/her to preach the gospel to the meek, the poor, the wealthy, and the afflicted. You have sent him/her to bind up and heal the brokenhearted, to proclaim liberty to the physical and spiritual captives, and to open the prison and the eyes of those who are bound. Thank You for the divine love You have shed abroad in his/her heart to love and care for the sheep.

No weapon formed against him/her will prosper, and any tongue that rises against him/her in judgment shall be shown to be in the wrong. I pray pastor holds fast and follows the pattern of wholesome and sound teaching in all faith and love, which is for us in Christ Jesus.

I pray that freedom of utterance is given to him/her to open his/her mouth boldly and courageously to speak the Word of God by the Spirit of God to help people. Thank You, Lord, for the added strength, which comes superhumanly, that You have given to him/ her _____.

According to the grace that we have been given, we as a church body shall stand behind and undergird our pastor in prayer. We the body grow up to know the whole truth and tell it in love—like Christ in everything. We take our lead from Jesus, who is the Source of everything we do. He keeps us in step with each other. His very breath and blood flow through us, nourishing us so that we will grow up healthy in God, robust in love. May we be filled with the knowledge of Your will in all wisdom and spiritual understanding. Dear Father, I also pray…

My Praise Report

My Boss and My Coworkers

Never let loyalty and kindness leave you!
Tie them around your neck as a reminder.
Write them deep within your heart. Then
you will find favor with both God and peo-
ple, and you will earn a good reputation.
PROVERBS 3:3-4 NLT

God's Word Speaking to Me

Lamentations 3:22-23 ◦ Ephesians 3:14-17, 20 ◦ 3 John 2
◦ 1 Timothy 2:1-3 ◦ Joshua 1:8 ◦ Psalm 5:12 ◦ Proverbs 2:7
◦ Proverbs 3:21 ◦ Psalm 115:14 ◦ Proverbs 8:12 ◦ Hebrews
6:14 ◦ 2 Thessalonians 1:12 ◦ Proverbs 21:1 ◦ Isaiah 33:6
◦ Philippians 4:19 ◦ James 1:2-5 ◦ Romans 12:17 NIV ◦
Ephesians 4:1-6, 25-32 ◦ 2 Peter 3:18

My Prayer

Decrees of Success for My Employer and My Coworkers

....
....
....
....
....
....
....
....
....
....
....

My Praise Report

....
....
....
....
....
....
....
....

My Nation and My World

*All nations will call you blessed, for you
will be a land sparkling with happiness.
These are the promises of the Lord Almighty.*
—MALACHI 3:12 TLB

*If my people who are called by my name will hum-
ble themselves and pray and seek my face and turn
from their wicked ways, I will hear from heaven
and will forgive their sins and restore their land.*
2 CHRONICLES 7:14 NLT

Blessed is the nation whose God is the Lord....
PSALM 33:12 NKJV

God's Word Speaking to Me

1 Timothy 2:1-3 ❖ Deuteronomy 28:10-11 ❖ Proverbs 2:10-12,21-22 ❖ Romans 8:37 AMPC ❖ Psalm 33:12 ❖ Proverbs 21:1 ❖ 2 Chronicles 7:14 NLT ❖ Leviticus 26:6 ❖ John 16:33 ❖ Luke 2:14 ❖ Psalm 34:14 ❖ Isaiah 60:2-3 ❖ Daniel 2:20-21 ❖ Romans 13:1 ❖ Matthew 6:9-10 ❖ Proverbs 14:34 ❖ Proverbs 9:10

My Prayer

Decrees for My Nation and My World

My Praise Report

Create Your Own Prayer

Today, the Lord is leading me to pray for...

....

....

....

....

....

....

....

....

God's Word Speaking to Me

....

....

....

....

....

....

....

....

My Prayer

My Praise Report

Create Your Own Prayer

Today, the Lord is leading me to pray for…

....
....
....
....
....
....
....

God's Word Speaking to Me

....
....
....
....
....
....
....
....
....

My Prayer

My Praise Report

Create Your Own Prayer

Today, the Lord is leading me to pray for...

....
....
....
....
....
....
....
....
....

God's Word Speaking to Me

....
....
....
....
....
....
....
....
....
....

My Prayer

My Praise Report

Create Your Own Prayer

Today, the Lord is leading me to pray for…

God's Word Speaking to Me

My Prayer

My Praise Report

Create Your Own Prayer

Today, the Lord is leading me to pray for...

....

....

....

....

....

....

....

....

God's Word Speaking to Me

....

....

....

....

....

....

....

....

....

My Prayer

....
....
....
....
....
....
....
....
....
....
....
....
....
....

My Praise Report

....
....
....
....
....

Create Your Own Prayer

Today, the Lord is leading me to pray for...

....

....

....

....

....

....

....

God's Word Speaking to Me

....

....

....

....

....

....

....

....

....

....

....

My Prayer

....
....
....
....
....
....
....
....
....
....
....
....
....
....

My Praise Report

....
....
....
....
....
....
....

Create Your Own Prayer

Today, the Lord is leading me to pray for...

....
....
....
....
....
....
....

God's Word Speaking to Me

....
....
....
....
....
....
....
....

My Prayer

My Praise Report

My Journal Notes